EXPLORING THE STATES

Michigan

THE GREAT LAKES STATE

by Amy Rechner

BLASTOFF! READERS 5

BELLWETHER MEDIA · MINNEAPOLIS, MN

Note to Librarians, Teachers, and Parents:

Blastoff! Readers are carefully developed by literacy experts and combine standards-based content with developmentally appropriate text.

Level 1 provides the most support through repetition of high-frequency words, light text, predictable sentence patterns, and strong visual support.

Level 2 offers early readers a bit more challenge through varied simple sentences, increased text load, and less repetition of high-frequency words.

Level 3 advances early-fluent readers toward fluency through increased text and concept load, less reliance on visuals, longer sentences, and more literary language.

Level 4 builds reading stamina by providing more text per page, increased use of punctuation, greater variation in sentence patterns, and increasingly challenging vocabulary.

Level 5 encourages children to move from "learning to read" to "reading to learn" by providing even more text, varied writing styles, and less familiar topics.

Whichever book is right for your reader, Blastoff! Readers are the perfect books to build confidence and encourage a love of reading that will last a lifetime!

This edition first published in 2014 by Bellwether Media, Inc.

No part of this publication may be reproduced in whole or in part without written permission of the publisher. For information regarding permission, write to Bellwether Media, Inc., Attention: Permissions Department, 5357 Penn Avenue South, Minneapolis, MN 55419.

Library of Congress Cataloging-in-Publication Data

Rechner, Amy.
 Michigan / by Amy Rechner.
  pages cm. – (Blastoff! readers. Exploring the states)
 Includes bibliographical references and index.
 Summary: "Developed by literacy experts for students in grades three through seven, this book introduces young readers to the geography and culture of Michigan"–Provided by publisher.
 ISBN 978-1-62617-021-6 (hardcover : alk. paper)
 1. Michigan–Juvenile literature. I. Title.
 F566.3.R43 2014
 977.4–dc23
                                                                    2013002390

Printed in the United States of America, North Mankato, MN.

Table of Contents

Where Is Michigan?

Michigan sits in two parts in the northern **Midwest**. The larger part is a **peninsula** shaped like a mitten. This is called the Lower Peninsula. To the north is the Upper Peninsula. Lake Michigan and Lake Huron separate these two landmasses.

Wisconsin lies southwest of the Upper Peninsula. The rest of the peninsula is surrounded mostly by Lakes Superior, Michigan, and Huron. Canada lies to the north of the Upper Peninsula and east of the Lower Peninsula. Indiana and Ohio are neighbors to the south. The state capital of Lansing stands in the middle of the Lower Peninsula.

Porcupine Mountains Wilderness State Park

Wisconsin

Lake
Superior

Canada

Lake
Michigan

Lake
Huron

Michigan

Grand Rapids

Lansing

Detroit

Indiana

Ohio

Native Americans were the first people to live in Michigan. French explorers arrived from Canada in the 1600s. They traded with the native tribes. England took control of this land after the French and Indian War. The United States gained the region after the **Revolutionary War**. Michigan became a state in 1837.

Andrew Jackson

Michigan

Toledo

Ohio

Did you know?
In 1835, Michigan and Ohio fought each other for the city of Toledo. President Andrew Jackson gave the city to Ohio. Michigan got the Upper Peninsula instead.

Michigan Timeline!

1618–1622: French explorer Étienne Brulé is the first European to visit Michigan.

1763: Native leader Chief Pontiac leads an unsuccessful attack on the British Army.

1783: The American colonies win independence from England. Michigan becomes the property of the new United States.

1825: The Erie Canal is completed. This opens up an easy shipping route from the Eastern United States to Michigan.

1837: Michigan becomes the twenty-sixth state.

1903: Henry Ford starts the Ford Motor Company in Detroit.

1914-1918: World War I creates new factory jobs. Many African Americans move to Michigan to work.

1959: A recording company called Motown Records opens in Detroit.

1967: Michigan struggles with violent race relations in Detroit, Flint, and other towns.

1974: Grand Rapids native Gerald Ford becomes the thirty-eighth President of the United States when Richard M. Nixon steps down.

Chief Pontiac

Henry Ford

Gerald Ford

The Land

Petoskey stone

fun fact !

Michigan is the only place where Petoskey stones are found. Their rare pattern was formed around 350 million years ago by a plant-like animal called coral.

Michigan's two peninsulas have very different **terrain**. The Lower Peninsula has high **bluffs** along its shores. Gentle hills roll into rich farmland in the south. Sand **dunes** line the western coast, and large lakes dot the northwest. Damp air from the **Great Lakes** brings snowy winters and sticky summers.

Michigan's Climate

average °F

spring
Low: 33°
High: 54°

summer
Low: 56°
High: 78°

fall
Low: 39°
High: 57°

winter
Low: 15°
High: 30°

Much of the Upper Peninsula is wilderness. It is covered with thick forests and rocky land. The Huron and Porcupine Mountains march along the Lake Superior shore. The Upper Peninsula has a much cooler climate than the Lower Peninsula, especially in the winter.

Porcupine Mountains Wilderness State Park

Porcupine Mountains Wilderness State Park covers the northwest corner of the Upper Peninsula. It boasts one of the largest uncut **hardwood** forests in the country. The Porcupine Mountains inside the park are two billion years old. They rise near the Lake Superior shore.

More than 90 waterfalls break up the park's rivers. Colorful striped rocks called agates are scattered on the beaches. Lake Superior's strong waves create ice **volcanoes** in the winter. Water freezes and builds up in a cone shape on the shore. Pounding waves spurt water up through the cone.

agates

ice volcano

Did you know?
The mountains in the Upper Peninsula get around 200 inches (508 centimeters) of snow each winter.

Wildlife

fox

muskrat

heron

Michigan's lands and waters provide shelter for a wide range of wildlife. Black bears and moose can be found in the northern forests. Deer roam both the Upper and Lower Peninsulas. The animals that once attracted fur traders to Michigan still live in the wild. Minks, muskrats, and foxes are just a few of these.

mink

Moose, gray wolves, and red squirrels are among the mammals that live on Michigan's Isle Royale. They had to travel at least 14 miles (22 kilometers) across Lake Superior to get there!

The state's lakes and rivers are filled with perch, bass, and walleye. Ducks, herons, and egrets live nearby. Owls, woodpeckers, and hundreds of songbirds fly through Michigan's wooded areas.

Landmarks

Michigan has many beautiful places to explore. Pictured Rocks National Lakeshore is a row of colorful sandstone cliffs in the Upper Peninsula. Formations such as Miners' Castle and Battleship Row were named for their shapes. In the Lower Peninsula is Sleeping Bear Dunes National Lakeshore. Its sand dunes tower more than 400 feet (120 meters) above the shore of Lake Michigan.

Dearborn is home to the Henry Ford Museum and Greenfield Village. The museum spotlights the history of **innovation** in America. Greenfield Village is filled with historic buildings that were moved or rebuilt there. One attraction is the Ford Rouge Factory. It is the only Detroit-area auto plant that holds public tours.

Miners' Castle

Sleeping Bear Dunes National Lakeshore

Greenfield Village

fun fact

The Wright brothers built the first successful airplane in their Ohio bicycle shop. The shop was later moved to Greenfield Village.

Detroit

Detroit is nicknamed Motor City. It has been the center of American auto production for more than 100 years.
In the early 1900s, African Americans came from the South to work in the auto plants. **Immigrants** from all over the world also traveled to Detroit for work. Today, more than 700,000 people of **diverse** backgrounds live in the city.

Charles H. Wright Museum

Detroit stands along the Detroit River on Michigan's southeastern border. Visitors enjoy long strolls on the city's RiverWalk. Bridges connect downtown Detroit to Canada and the island park of Belle Isle. Families can tour the Detroit Zoo and the city's many museums.

Working

Did you know?

Michigan produces more blueberries and tart cherries than any other state.

Michigan was built by hard work. In its early years, the state's trees, copper, and iron attracted lumberjacks and miners. Today many Michiganders are farmers or factory workers. Farmers grow corn, soybeans, and sugar beets. They also raise cattle and hogs. Workers in factories make furniture, food products, and cars. More cars are made in Michigan than in any other state.

Many Michiganders have **service jobs**. They work at hospitals, banks, and other businesses. **Tourists** flock to the natural beauty of the state's parks and lakeshores. Michiganders serve them at hotels, restaurants, and other places that welcome visitors.

fun fact

Henry Ford's 1908 Model T was the first car that average Americans could afford. In 1925, it sold for less than $300!

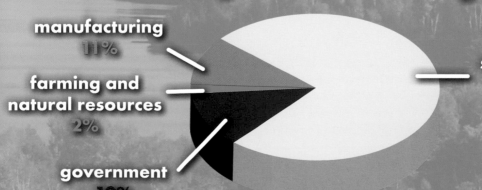

Where People Work in Michigan

manufacturing
11%

farming and
natural resources
2%

services
75%

government
12%

Playing

Did you know?

Michigan State University and the University of Michigan have a strong football rivalry. Each year, the Spartans and the Wolverines play each other for the Paul Bunyan Trophy.

Michigan is the place for year-round outdoor fun. Lake Michigan beaches draw visitors in the summer. More than 11,000 inland lakes offer swimming, boating, and fishing. Hiking trails across the state's countryside are busy during all seasons.

The snowy mountains of the Upper Peninsula are a skier's paradise in winter. Cross-country skiing and **snowmobiling** are also popular. Ice hockey is a favorite sport to play and watch. The Detroit Red Wings have a loyal following. Detroit is also home to the Lions football team and Tigers baseball. College sports fans root for the University of Michigan Wolverines and the Michigan State Spartans.

fun fact

Michiganders find thrills and chills at the yearly International 500 Snowmobile Race. This 500-mile (805-kilometer) race is held on an oval track. It is often described as "NASCAR on ice."

Cornish Pasties

Ingredients:

Filling:
2 cups diced potatoes
1 large onion, diced
1 cup diced rutabaga
1/2 cup diced carrot
1 1/2 teaspoon salt
1/2 teaspoon pepper
1 1/2 pound coarsely ground lean beef

Crust:
6 cups flour
1 tablespoon salt
1 pound shortening

Directions:

1. In a large bowl, mix all filling ingredients and set aside.

2. In a medium bowl, mix flour and salt. Then cut in shortening until crumbly.

3. Divide dough into 6 equal rounds and roll out flat. Place one-sixth of the filling in the middle of each crust. Fold over and crimp edges.

4. Place pasties on an ungreased cookie sheet and bake at 350°F for about 75 minutes.

coney

Many of the nation's favorite foods were created in Michigan. In Battle Creek, the Kellogg brothers made the first breakfast cereal flakes. They are now enjoyed as Kellogg's Corn Flakes. A Detroit man named James Vernor created one of the first soft drinks. Vernors Ginger Ale is still sold in Michigan.

Coney Island hot dogs were also born in Michigan. A "coney" is an all-beef hot dog topped with beef chili, onions, and mustard. The Upper Peninsula is famous for its Cornish pasties. These pastry pockets are filled with meat, potatoes, and other vegetables. After a hearty meal, Michiganders love to bake tart cherries into cakes, pies, and other desserts.

Festivals

Michiganders like to celebrate when the weather is warm. The town of Holland honors its Dutch heritage with the Tulip Time Festival in May. Blooming tulips, parades, and Dutch crafts welcome spring. The National Cherry Festival in Traverse City celebrates the cherry harvest in July. Events include an air show, a parade, and a cherry pit-spitting contest.

Michigan's history is brought to life at Fort Michilimackinac in Mackinaw City. Each Memorial Day weekend, a historical pageant is held to remember Pontiac's War in 1763. Actors in costume recreate the fight between Pontiac's men and the British Army.

National Cherry Festival

Tulip Time Festival

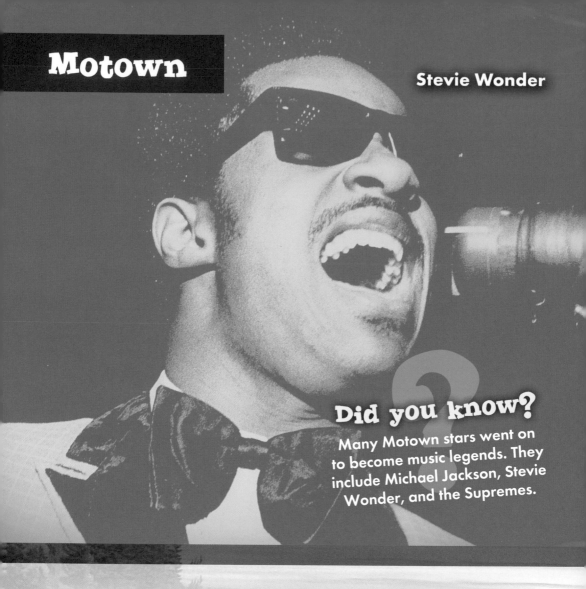

Motown

Stevie Wonder

Did you know?

Many Motown stars went on to become music legends. They include Michael Jackson, Stevie Wonder, and the Supremes.

Detroit songwriter Berry Gordy, Jr. started the Motown Record Corporation in 1959. It changed American pop music forever. Motown's records featured African-American musicians. They performed songs that combined jazz, **gospel**, and pop styles. People loved the upbeat rhythms and smooth **harmonies**. The Motown sound became hugely popular in America.

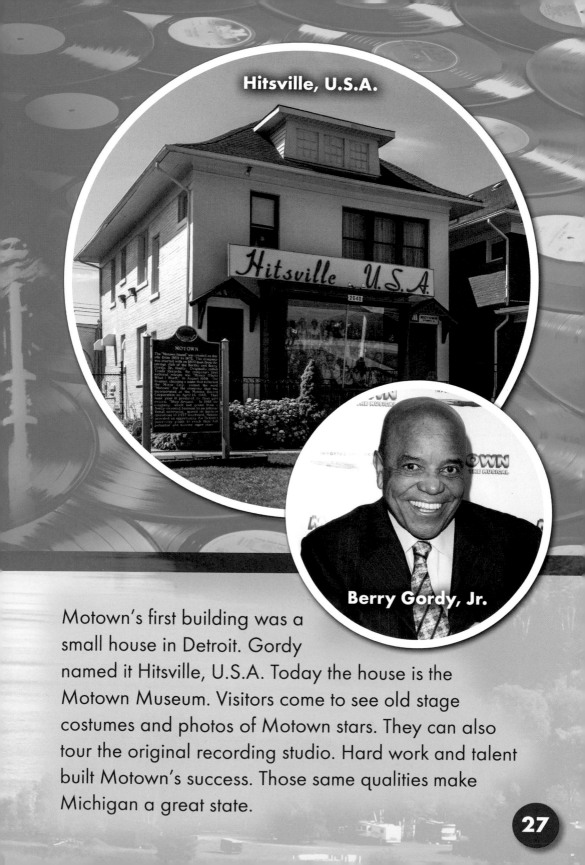

Hitsville, U.S.A.

Berry Gordy, Jr.

Motown's first building was a small house in Detroit. Gordy named it Hitsville, U.S.A. Today the house is the Motown Museum. Visitors come to see old stage costumes and photos of Motown stars. They can also tour the original recording studio. Hard work and talent built Motown's success. Those same qualities make Michigan a great state.

Fast Facts About Michigan

Michigan's Flag

Michigan's dark blue flag features the state coat of arms in the center. An elk and a moose hold a shield that shows a man on a grassy peninsula. Above the shield, a bald eagle holds an olive branch and arrows. The state's mottos surround the coat of arms.

State Flower
apple blossom

State Nicknames:	Wolverine State Great Lakes State
State Motto:	*Si Quaeris Peninsulam Amoenam, Circumspice*; "If You Seek a Pleasant Peninsula, Look About You"
Year of Statehood:	1837
Capital City:	Lansing
Other Major Cities:	Detroit, Grand Rapids
Population:	9,883,640 (2010)
Area:	96,713 square miles (250,486 square kilometers); Michigan is the 11th largest state.
Major Industries:	car manufacturing, tourism, farming, mining
Natural Resources:	lumber, freshwater, copper, iron
State Government:	110 representatives; 38 senators
Federal Government:	14 representatives; 2 senators
Electoral Votes:	16

State Animal
white-tailed deer

State Bird
American robin

Glossary

bluffs—cliffs or steep banks

diverse—made up of many different types or coming from many different backgrounds

dunes—hills of sand

gospel—a type of music often characterized by songs of praise, strong vocals, and repetition

Great Lakes—five large freshwater lakes on the border between the United States and Canada

hardwood—a tree with broad leaves, such as an oak or a maple

harmonies—combinations of notes or chords that are pleasing to the ear

immigrants—people who leave one country to live in another country

innovation—the development of new ideas, methods, or things

Midwest—a region of 12 states in the north-central United States

native—originally from a specific place

peninsula—a section of land that extends out from a larger piece of land and is almost completely surrounded by water

Revolutionary War—the war between 1775 and 1783 in which the United States fought for independence from Great Britain

service jobs—jobs that perform tasks for people or businesses

snowmobiling—the sport of driving snowmobiles; snowmobiles are vehicles that move quickly over snow.

terrain—the surface features of an area of land

tourists—people who travel to visit another place

volcanoes—holes in the earth; when a volcano erupts, hot, melted rock called lava shoots out; ice volcanoes are so named because they resemble real volcanoes.

To Learn More

AT THE LIBRARY

Downey, Tika. *Michigan: The Great Lakes State.* New York, N.Y.: PowerKids Press, 2010.

El Nabli, Dina. *Henry Ford: Putting the World on Wheels.* New York, N.Y.: HarperCollins, 2008.

Wyckoff, Edwin Brit. *The Cornflake King: W.K. Kellogg and His Amazing Cereal.* Berkeley Heights, N.J.: Enslow Elementary, 2011.

ON THE WEB

Learning more about Michigan is as easy as 1, 2, 3.

1. Go to www.factsurfer.com.

2. Enter "Michigan" into the search box.

3. Click the "Surf" button and you will see a list of related Web sites.

With factsurfer.com, finding more information is just a click away.

Index

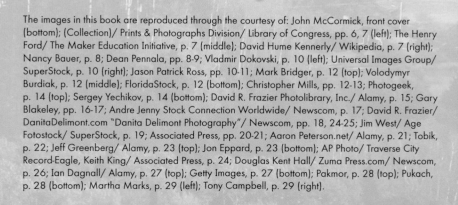

The images in this book are reproduced through the courtesy of: John McCormick, front cover (bottom); (Collection)/ Prints & Photographs Division/ Library of Congress, pp. 6, 7 (left); The Henry Ford/ The Maker Education Initiative, p. 7 (middle); David Hume Kennerly/ Wikipedia, p. 7 (right); Nancy Bauer, p. 8; Dean Pennala, pp. 8-9; Vladmir Dokovski, p. 10 (left); Universal Images Group/ SuperStock, p. 10 (right); Jason Patrick Ross, pp. 10-11; Mark Bridger, p. 12 (top); Volodymyr Burdiak, p. 12 (middle); FloridaStock, p. 12 (bottom); Christopher Mills, pp. 12-13; Photogeek, p. 14 (top); Sergey Yechikov, p. 14 (bottom); David R. Frazier Photolibrary, Inc./ Alamy, p. 15; Gary Blakeley, pp. 16-17; Andre Jenny Stock Connection Worldwide/ Newscom, p. 17; David R. Frazier/ DanitaDelimont.com "Danita Delimont Photography"/ Newscom, pp. 18, 24-25; Jim West/ Age Fotostock/ SuperStock, p. 19; Associated Press, pp. 20-21; Aaron Peterson.net/ Alamy, p. 21; Tobik, p. 22; Jeff Greenberg/ Alamy, p. 23 (top); Jon Eppard, p. 23 (bottom); AP Photo/ Traverse City Record-Eagle, Keith King/ Associated Press, p. 24; Douglas Kent Hall/ Zuma Press.com/ Newscom, p. 26; Ian Dagnall/ Alamy, p. 27 (top); Getty Images, p. 27 (bottom); Pakmor, p. 28 (top); Pukach, p. 28 (bottom); Martha Marks, p. 29 (left); Tony Campbell, p. 29 (right).